Mastering Italic Calligraphy

BOOKS BY ARTHUR BAKER

CALLIGRAPHY

CALLIGRAPHIC ALPHABETS

THE ROMAN ALPHABET

DANCE OF THE PEN

THE SCRIPT ALPHABET

CALLIGRAPHIC INITIALS

HISTORIC CALLIGRAPHIC ALPHABETS

CALLIGRAPHIC ORNAMENTS AND FLOURISHES

ARTHUR BAKER'S COPYBOOK OF
  RENAISSANCE CALLIGRAPHY
  (Mercator's Italic Hand)

CHANCERY CURSIVE, STROKE BY STROKE
  An Arthur Baker Calligraphy Manual

CALLIGRAPHIC CUT PAPER DESIGNS

CELTIC UNCIAL, STROKE BY STROKE
  (The Book of Kells) An Arthur Baker Calligraphy Manual

ARTHUR BAKER'S COPYBOOK OF
  LATINIZED GOTHIC CALLIGRAPHY
  (Roots of the Bauhaus) An Arthur Baker Calligraphy Manual

FULL COLOR PAPER AIRPLANES

SQUARE CAPITALS, STROKE BY STROKE
  An Arthur Baker Calligraphy Manual

CALLIGRAPHIC SWASH CAPITALS

BRUSH CALLIGRAPHY

SPLIT PEN CALLIGRAPHY

ARTHUR BAKER'S ENCYCLOPEDIA
  OF CALLIGRAPHY STYLES

THE CALLIGRAPHIC ART OF ARTHUR BAKER

FOUNDATIONAL CALLIGRAPHY MANUAL

Arthur Baker

Mastering Italic Calligraphy

CHARLES SCRIBNER'S SONS/NEW YORK

Library of Congress Catalog Number 85-62301
ISBN 0-684-18214-9

Published simultaneously in Canada by Collier
Macmillan Canada, Inc.—Copyright under
the Berne Convention.

1 3 5 7 9 11 13 15 17 19 Q/P 20 18 16 14 12 10 8 6 4 2

Printed in the United States of America.

INTRODUCTION

Let's begin by stressing the title of this book and a word that has been chosen with precision—*mastering*. This book is devoted to mastering the art and craft of what has come to be called Italic Calligraphy. The concept of the master of a trade has an old-fashioned ring to modern ears. We think of golf, chess, brewing, and schoolmasters, but there were—and are—writing masters as well.

Of writing masters there were many in the period which first saw a codification of the cursive, flowing style of penmanship in Italy. Scribes who worked for the papal chancery office, recording church communications during the Renaissance, became competitively vain about their expertise in the running hand known as *corsiva cancellerescha*—chancery cursive. Ludovico Vincentino de Arrighi was first off the mark with a book that demonstrated his brilliant, detailed instructions on how to write the "Italic" hand; *La Operina*, published in Rome in 1522, was the first writing book. The literacy that accompanied the wide availability of printed books, begun in mid-fifteenth–century Europe, created a demand for such manuals, and the now-classic styles of Tagliente, Mercator, Palatino, and other scribes were published and widely used.

Most of these manuals are readily available in facsimile today, and it is to be hoped that they are familiar to the scribe who seeks, with the aid of Arthur Baker's method of building the letters in carefully constructed sequential drawings, to master the italic form. If you have attempted to follow the classic examples, you have undoubtedly struggled with trying to understand the holding and manipulation of the pen. Few of the classic plates provide descriptions of construction method; most show only the diversity and brilliance of the masters' styles. That lack is more than made up for in this book with its novel approach to detailed instruction in the italic hand.

As a contemporary master of letterform, Arthur Baker has no peers. One would have to reexamine the output of the Renaissance scribes to see equivalents. The beauty and brilliance of Baker's artistic gift is evident on every page of the two dozen books he has issued over the past fifteen years; in his manuals of instruction the ingeniously simple method of showing his own hand creating each stroke of each minuscule and capital letter is unique and is of unique and immediate help to the student in learning how to create the graceful flow of the Italic hand. Arthur Baker has here created the definitive manual of Italic calligraphy.

William Hogarth
Sea Cliff, New York

BASIC SUPPLIES
AND INSTRUCTIONS

The basic supplies for calligraphy are simple and easy to find in a local craft or art supply store. You will need a broad-edged pen, ink that is compatible with the pen you are using, a variety of papers, a ruler, pencils, an eraser such as the Magic Rub white rubber eraser, and masking or drafting tape. These materials are described in detail below.

Pens

I recommend that the beginner learn calligraphy with a large-point pen, either 1/4″ or 1/2″ wide. The Coit company makes a series of pens in this size range, as well as larger and smaller sizes. A large pen helps the beginner see the letters clearly, making them easier to analyze. The instruction plates in this manual were drawn with a Coit pen. The nib, or point, and the holder come as a single unit.

Other acceptable pens are the Speedball C-series, pen point size C-O, and the Brause, point size 5 mm. With these points you will need a pen holder. Most art supply stores that sell pen points also sell a variety of holders.

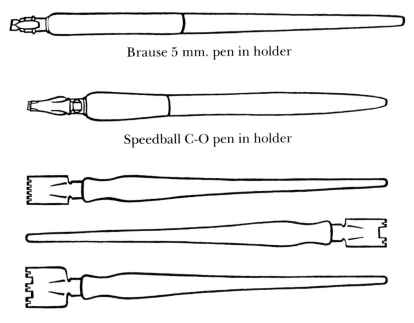

Brause 5 mm. pen in holder

Speedball C-O pen in holder

Coit pens. Top pen makes a solid line; the bottom two make split lines.

"Italic" fountain pens such as Platignum and Osmiroid have a convenient inkwell inside the pen; however, they can use only water-soluble inks. Also, the fountain pens have relatively small points and so are not the best choice for calligraphy practice. If you wish to use one, write with the largest point size available. For small calligraphy, the Speedball or Brause small point sizes (C-1 to C-6 and ½ mm. to 4 mm.) are best.

Speedball steel brushes are not good for this kind of work, and the Wm. Mitchell pens are too flexible. I do not advise using them in the beginning.

Left-handers can usually find left-oblique pens. If not, it is possible to grind right-oblique pens to a flat angle on a hard Arkansas stone, which is available in hardware stores. The Coit pen can be used ambidextrously because it is flat-edged.

The different types of pens should be filled in different ways. To fill the Coit pen, pour the ink into a small jar to a depth of ½" to ¾". Dip the pen into the ink, and tap it against the side of the jar to release the excess. With Brause or Speedball pens, fill the reservoir on the top of the pen with the dropper in the top of the ink bottle, or use a small brush. Be careful not to overload the pen with ink, or it will form a blot when you begin to write. It is a good idea to make the first stroke after each fill on a piece of scrap paper, in case there is too much ink in the pen.

Follow the manufacturer's instructions for filling fountain pens. Be sure to use the kind of ink the manufacturer recommends, or the inside of the pen will become permanently clogged.

After using the Coit, Speedball, or Brause points, wipe them dry. If after several uses, the ink accumulates and clogs the points, soak them in ammonia for a few minutes, scrub with a toothbrush reserved for this purpose, rinse with water, and dry. Clean fountain pens according to the manufacturer's directions.

Ink

It is preferable to use black, waterproof ink, and there are many brands to choose from. Higgins Engrossing Ink, Pelikan Black Drawing Ink, Grumbacher India Ink, and Winsor Newton Black Drawing Ink are all excellent. Sumi ink that is already mixed with water is inexpensive and very black but will corrode pen points. Some inks—such as "extra dense" ink—contain shellac, and if you dilute them, a few drops of ammonia should be added.

If the hairlines seem thick when you are writing, you probably need to thin the ink. Some inks, like Pelikan Drawing Ink, can be thinned quite a bit, but be sure that the ink still dries solid black after it has been diluted.

Colored inks and dyes are beautiful and easy to use, but you should be aware that most of these colors will fade quickly if exposed to sunlight. If you wish to do a finished piece of calligraphy using color, it is best to use thinned designer's gouache (rhymes with wash). Gouache is a dense watercolor pigment that comes in a tube. Squeeze some paint from the tube into a small dish or watercolor palette, and mix with a few drops of water, using a brush. Add as much water as you need to make the paint thin but not runny. Use the brush to fill the pen.

Work Surface

It is easier to do calligraphy on an inclined surface. There are many fine drawing tables available that fold up flat when not in use for those who have limited space.

It is also easy to improvise a substitute drawing table. Simply prop a board on a table with a stack of books under the back edge. The angle of the board can be varied by adding or subtracting books. To keep the board from slipping off the table, tape a thin strip of wood to the table's edge.

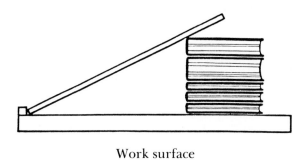

Work surface

Paper

The paper you use for practice should be inexpensive enough so that you do not hesitate to use all you want. The papers marketed as calligraphy paper with printed guidelines are often very costly and no better for practice than regular paper.

The size and surface quality of practice paper will depend on the size and kind of pen you are using. A large pen such as the Coit is most suited to 18″ × 24″ bond or drawing paper. The Grumbacher Big Drawing Paper Pad is good; it has 100 sheets that you can cut in half for practice if you wish. The Big Pad paper is also good for Speedball C-O and Brause 5 mm. pen practice. However, for these smaller pens and for fountain pens, you may prefer to use tracing paper in 9″ × 12″ or 11″ × 14″ pads because it is smooth and translucent. Avoid vellum paper, which is very expensive.

For finished pieces of calligraphy there are many fine papers. You can match the mood of a quotation, alphabet, poem, or poster to a beautifully colored or textured paper. For white papers, you can use the Grumbacher paper, or for higher quality you can use Bristol board, which comes in many thicknesses (1 to 4 ply) and two finishes, plate (slick) or kid finish (velvety). The varieties of colored papers are endless, in nearly every price range from 50¢ to $6.00 a sheet. Less expensive papers include Strathmore charcoal and Crescent drawing. The Crescent paper has matching mat boards that you may find suited to some projects. Some higher-priced papers are Ingres, Fabriano, Morilla, and Moriki (this beautiful Japanese rice paper comes in nearly 30 colors). Every kind of paper has different qualities and properties, so you should experiment with all of them.

Practice Techniques

When you know the size of the pen you will be practicing with, you should make a master guideline sheet for that pen. This will save you the trouble of ruling each sheet individually. Tape the master guidelines to your work surface, then tape a blank sheet over the ruled sheet. You will be able to see the guidelines well enough so that it will not be necessary to rule them on every sheet.

You may find that vertical guidelines are helpful for practice; they can be placed every 1″ to 2″. The pen will write more smoothly if you pad the work surface with several sheets of paper under the guidelines.

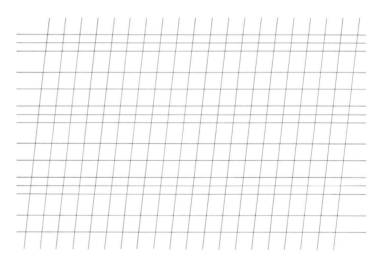

Ruled guideline sample

THE LETTERS

The basic measure of letter height is the height of the minuscule, or lowercase, x. The x-height of the Italic alphabet shown in the instruction plates is 5 times the width of the pen used to write it. The length of the ascenders and descenders in this alphabet is 4 pen widths, while the height of the majuscule, uppercase or capital letter, is less than the height of the ascender. It is 7 pen widths high from the baseline, and the capital proportion is independent of the minuscule—that is, the center of the capital falls below the upper x-height line. The Italic alphabet is written on a slanted angle, approximately 7° to the right.

While the instruction plates and sample alphabets in the ruled boxes hold to the ratio of 5 pen widths to the minuscule and 7 pen widths to the majuscule, this should not be regarded as a hard and fast law of this alphabet style. The art plates at the end of this book freely interpret the Italic alphabet characters into different weights or different pen width to x-height ratios. These variations show the endless design possibilities inherent in this alphabet.

The Italic alphabet is a descendant of the classical Roman alphabet and has a distinct technical relationship to it. The formal Italic calligraphy taught in this book is the manuscript form of this alphabet style; it is very different from the simplified Renaissance teaching of Italic handwriting with a fixed-pen angle technique.

The first-century Roman alphabet was written with a broad pen, manipulated over the course of writing each stroke in a logical related system. The basic strokes, in their simplest form in the letters *I* and *O*, delineate the principles that appear in all of the other letters. The *I* begins with the pen held at a 0° angle, then rotated to approximately 45° at the center of the letter, then back to 0° at the end of the stroke. The *O* is divided into two strokes that follow the same principles. The left side of the *O* begins with the pen held at a 45° angle, rotating to 0° at the end of the stroke. The right side of the *O* begins at the top with a 0° angle and ends with a 45° pen angle. This harmonious relationship between the two basic strokes unifies the entire alphabet as it is interpreted throughout all the letters.

Comparison of pen manipulation in classical Roman majuscules (left) and Italic majuscules (right)

The Italic alphabet shown in this book incorporates two versions of the Roman principle. The capital letters maintain virtually the same pattern of manipulation, while the minuscule letters have a slightly modified angle change.

The angle change for the minuscule *i* is approximately 25° to 50° to 25°. The curved strokes of the *o* maintain the relationship, with the right side changing from 50° to 25° and the left side beginning with 25° and terminating with 50°. The instructional plates provide the solutions for

Pen manipulation in Italic minuscules

the application of these principles to each of the rest of the letters, both majuscule and minuscule.

Even though both the majuscules and minuscules are written with the same pen, this difference in manipulation will cause the majuscules to appear bolder. This is an appropriate design solution to the problem of Italic capitals, which causes them to be slightly more pronounced in texts and not appear too small.

The Technique

The technique of pen manipulation involves the coordination of the fingers, hand, wrist, and arm in a continuous, unified motion. It also involves active observation on the part of the writer; although the technique can become very natural, the writer's intellect must be constantly engaged in the creation of the letters.

The pen is held comfortably in the hand, like a pencil. Try to keep your hand relaxed, not gripping the pen tightly. The angle of the pen nib is changed by turning the pen's position in the hand, accomplished by moving the fingers as shown in the illustration. The pen is turned by the thumb and forefinger at the beginning and end of the strokes, especially

Holding the pen

at serif junctures where the pivot is more pronounced. Do not try to twirl the pen like a Chinese brush, without changing the position of the pen in hand, because then your letters will not have the necessary strength and internal control of the line.

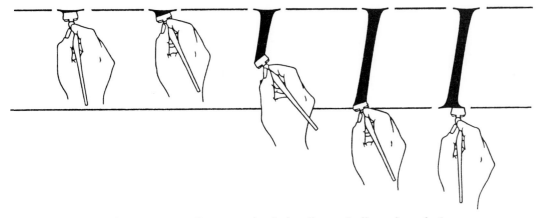

The sequence of pen manipulation for an Italic majuscule *I*.
Note the change of the position of the pen in the hand.

The wrist and arm are both involved when doing pen manipulation; the hand must move at the wrist to permit the pen to turn in the hand, and the arm provides the motion for each stroke. Do not try to write without moving your arm. Even small writing will involve some arm movement. This simultaneous motion of the fingers, hand, wrist, and arm will produce solid, strong letters, and you will find that your calligraphy is easier to control.

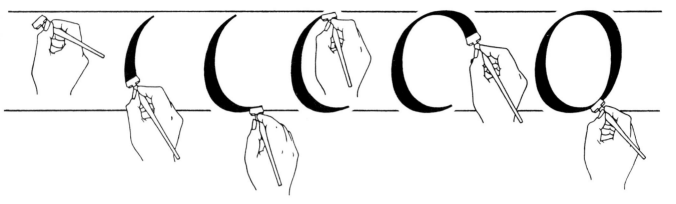

The sequence of pen manipulation for an Italic majuscule *O*. Note the change of the position of the hand. Below, the sequence for writing the serif stroke of the *E* and *F*. The same stroke is used on the *C* and *G*.

While it is good to follow the models for this alphabet when you are learning, do not be intimidated by them. The freedom you will gain when you understand pen manipulation will permit you to experiment, to modify the expression in your letter-forms to reflect your own sense of design and beauty. As long as you incorporate the pen manipulation principles explained here, your work will have an intrinsic harmony that will justify your experimentation and personal expression.

The Serifs

The serifs of the majuscules of the Italic alphabet are written similarly to the serifs on classical Roman capitals. When writing the serif on the top of a letter, slide the pen across the top to form the right side of the serif, then slide it back to the left and begin the stroke as illustrated in the plates. When finishing a stroke with a full serif, end the stroke toward the right side, then slide the pen to the left to form the left side. You should not have to add thickening to the letter stroke where it meets the serif if you have properly written the body of the letter.

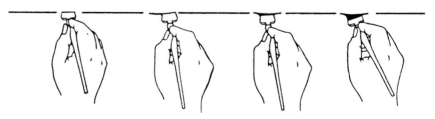

Forming the serif at the top of the letter

The serifs on the minuscule are formed by a slight lead-in stroke at the same angle that the letter begins, 25°. The exit serifs are formed in the same manner, leading out of the letter.

The Spacing

When you are writing words, every letter should seem to be exactly in the middle of the letters to its right and left. This is often an optical judgement, where you must be aware of the forms of each individual letter—whether it has a straight side, a curved side, or an open side. Generally speaking, two letters that have straight sides, such as the minuscule *i* and *n*, will have more space between then than any pair of letters in your text will have. Two curved letters, such as the minuscules *o* and *c*, will have the least space between them. A curved letter next to a straight letter would be closer than two straight letters, but not as close as two curved letters. In a continuous text, you should try to make the space between two straight stroke letters and two curved stroke letters appear to be the same. You can practice spacing letters by writing lines of letters such as *ininin*, or *ioioio*, or *oooooo*, staying aware of the space between the letters by checking back to the first letters you have written and comparing the spaces.

Letters such as the minuscules *k, c, s, x, v,* and *z* each present individual problems in text writing. Because one or the other of the sides of these letters is open, they must be spaced slightly closer to the letter on the open side than two letters with straight sides would be spaced. In a formal Italic, this problem can be solved by touching the letters in this situation. For example, in the word *quick*, the *c* lower stroke is brought up to touch the side of the *k* straight stroke. The *w* in the word *brown* presents this problem

Letter spacing

on both sides—with a curved letter (*o*) on the left and a straight letter (*n*) on the right. Note how the *w* touches the *o* and the *n* touches the *w*. Also examine the spaces between the *ow* and the *wn*. If these three letters were isolated from the rest of the word, the *w* would appear to be centered between the other two letters.

In the word *brown*, the *r* does not touch either the *b* or the *o*. While this is not an inflexible rule, you must always be alert when writing minuscules not to touch letters when their connection might obscure one or the other of the letter's forms. The minuscule is particularly susceptible to ambiguity, and so if there is any question about the legibility of the word, it is safer not to let the letters touch.

Letter spacing

The same general principles apply to the majuscules of formal Italic calligraphy. You should always keep in mind that the letters are your servants, and we have the freedom within the limits of form and legibility to alter or vary them to suit our needs. An example of this would be to shorten the crossbar of the *T* as it touches the *H* in the word *THE*, or the variation of the crossbar in the second *THE*.

The space between words is usually equivalent to the space inside the *o* (the *counter* space).

The Numerals

The numerals are similar in calligraphic technique to the letters. The numeral *1* is similar to the minuscule *i*, though a little taller; the zero is like the *o*, and so on. Two types of numerals are shown here: *lining*, which are so called because they do not have ascenders or descenders, and *old style,* which have some ascenders and descenders.

$$1234567890$$

Lining numerals

$$1234567890$$

Old style numerals

The
quick brown fox
jumps over
the lazy dog

THE
QUICK BROWN
FOX
JUMPS OVER
THE LAZY
DOG

The Swashes and Flourishes

The Italic alphabet is very receptive to a variety of swashes and flourishes. During the Renaissance these letters were extensively flourished in writing masters' books. Flourishes require tasteful application, but they can be used to great effect in many different contexts. It is important when adding swashes and flourishes to letters that you not obscure the form of the letter with the flourish. When you become accomplished in the art of flourishing, you will find that you can add flourishes in places other than those indicated here.

You should write the flourish lines with the same kind of pen manipulation that you would use when writing a letter. This way, the integration of the form is maintained. Swashes and flourishes provide an opportunity for expression and can be fun to write as well as to see.

The minuscule is able to support extensive swashing and flourishing. The primary vehicles for embellishment are the ascenders and descenders, although the x-height minuscules are capable of some rather exciting treatments, as the illustrations show. In the instruction pages the ascenders and descenders are shown in their simplest form; however, in these illustrations some of the many possibilities for variation are presented. Keep in mind that the minuscule form is more easily distorted or lost with the addition of flourishes than the majuscule, and so it must be treated more conservatively.

This illustration shows simple ascender solutions. The *f* is the only lowercase letter that has an ascender and a descender; however, the ascender must not be distorted too much as it is an important element of the letterform.

Minuscule ascender flourishes

These descenders are given enthusiastic treatment. The *f* has a large flourish, as do the four *g*'s (which represent the two forms that the Italic minuscule *g* can take). The *p*'s are fairly conservative, while the *g*'s are more elaborate, representing both forms of *g*. The *y* shows only one of many possible variations.

The first *a* and the *m* have a similar treatment, which can also apply to *n* and *h*. The flourish on the *n* can be used on *m* and *h*. The beginning flourish on the *v* can be used on *y* or *w*, however if used on *w*, it is wiser not to use the loop shown on this *w* together with it.

Minuscule descender flourishes

Minuscule flourishes on letters that do not have descenders
or ascenders

Minuscule ligatures

The combination of the letters *ct* and *st*, which occur often in the English
language, may be connected by means of a ligature as shown above. The
ligature may be simple or very elaborate.

This set of eight *A*'s demonstrates the wide variety of potential treatments of swash capitals. Every part of the letter can be given imaginative treatment, even the crossbar. Note that even the most complex of the letters is still readable as *A*.

Eight variations of the majuscule *A*

Majuscules with a variety of flourish treatments

The Italic majuscule alphabet presents exciting challenges for swashing and flourishing. Many of the letters have similar structural elements that can be treated with the same kinds of flourishes. An example of this is the set of letters, *B, D, E. F, H, K, R,* and *P,* each of which has a vertical left side and can therefore be flourished at the top left corner. Flourishes at the bottom left corner must be handled very carefully, however, as they can easily distort the letter into an unreadable form. The loop on the bottom left of the *E,* which is similar to the *L,* is an acceptable solution to this problem. This loop may be used on the *D* also. The letter *M* may be given many varieties of swashes, as may the *N* and *X.*

The Ampersands

The ampersand is an ancient convention for tieing together the letters *et,* the Latin word for "and." It began as a ligature, but has evolved into many versions over the centuries, and is now an accepted symbol. The three ampersands in the top row were all in use during the Renaissance and were often beautifully flourished.

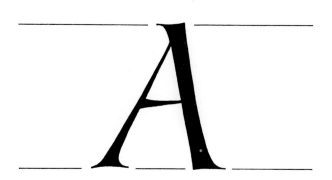

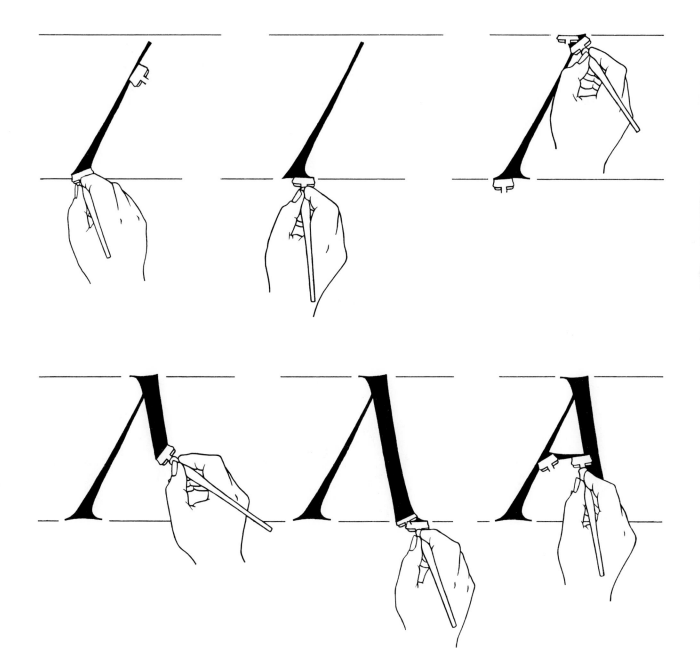

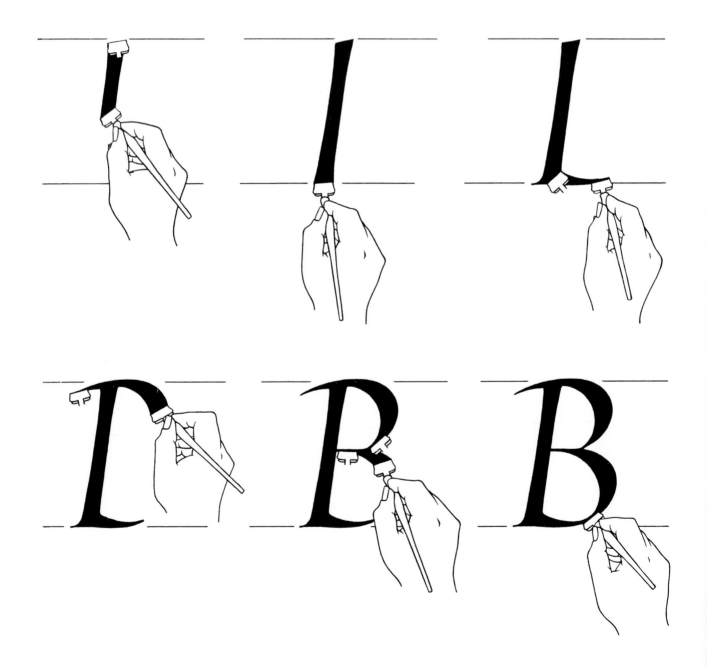

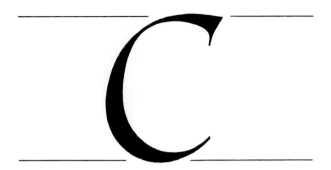

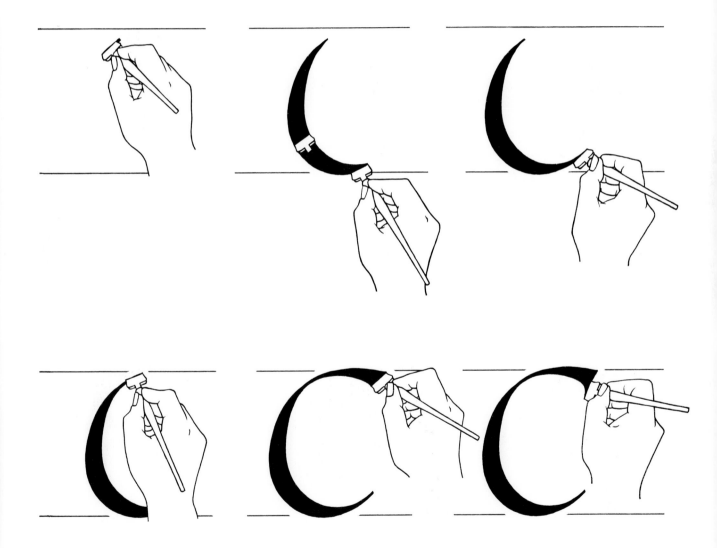

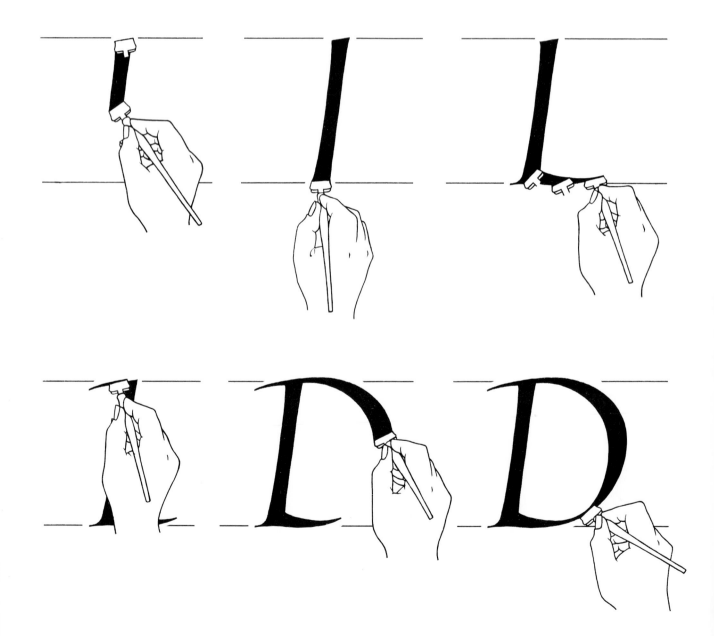

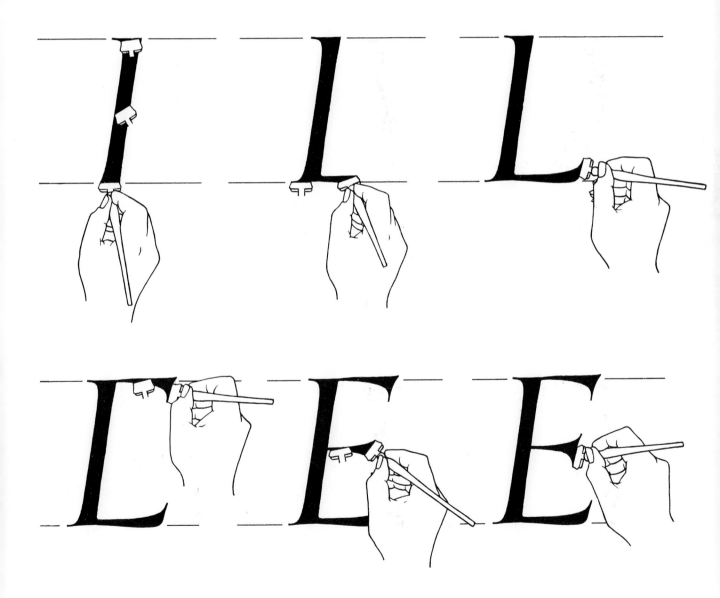

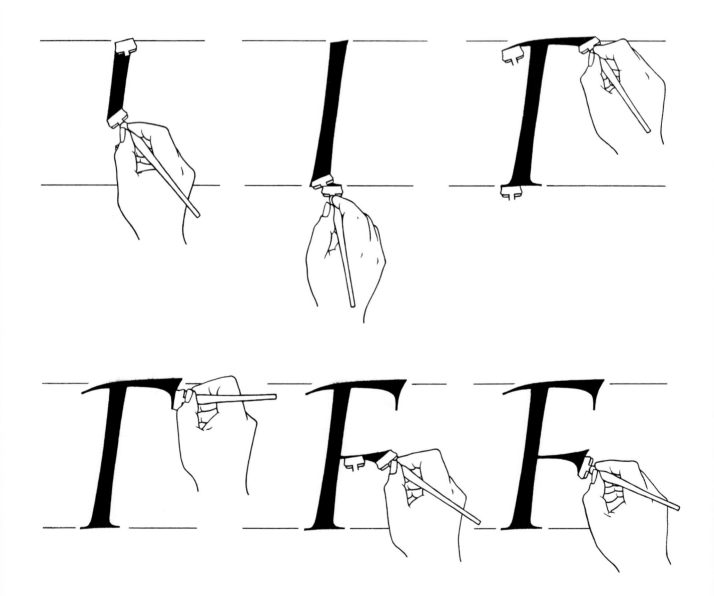

G

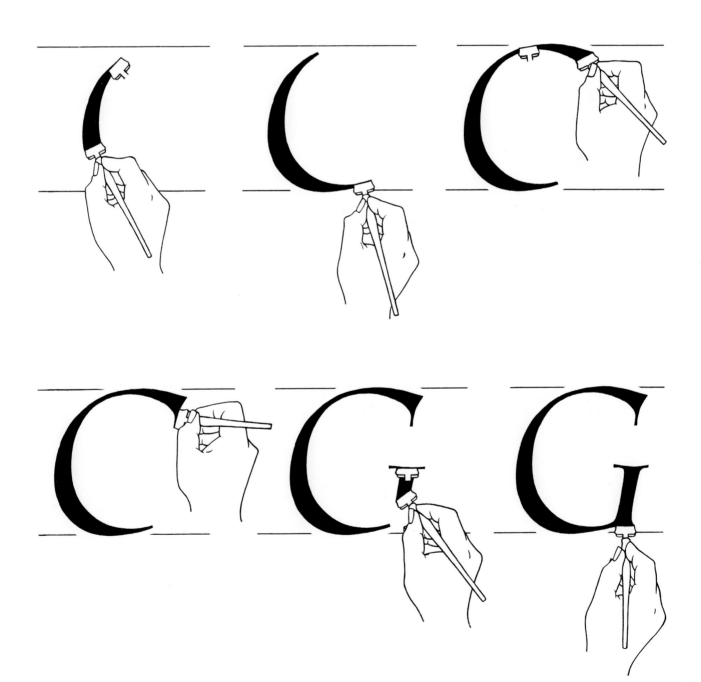

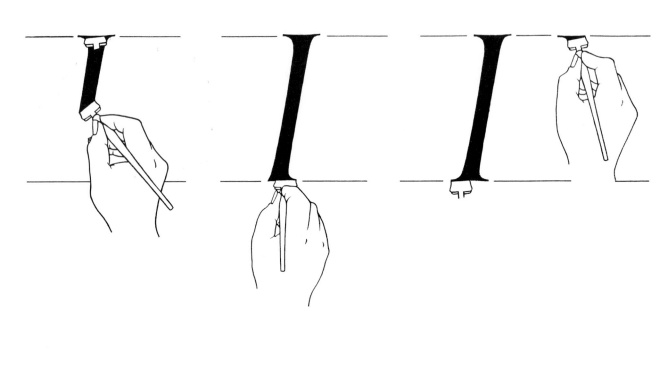

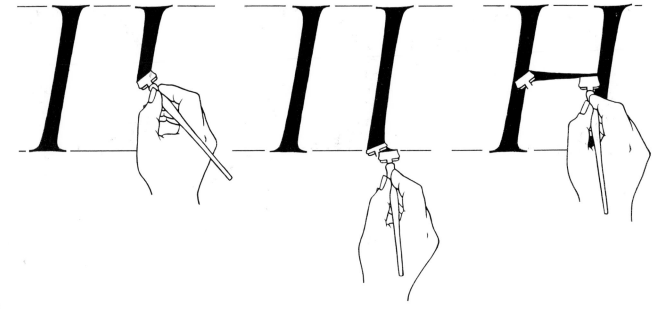

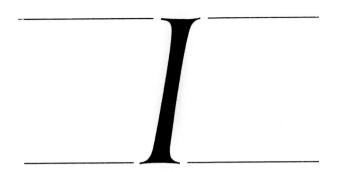

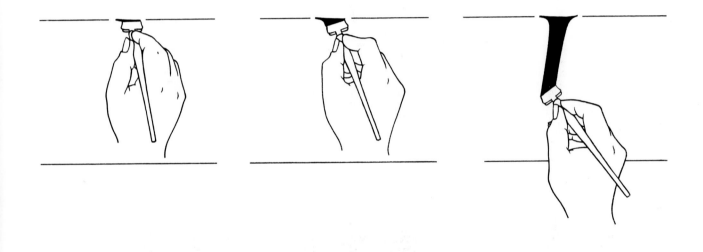

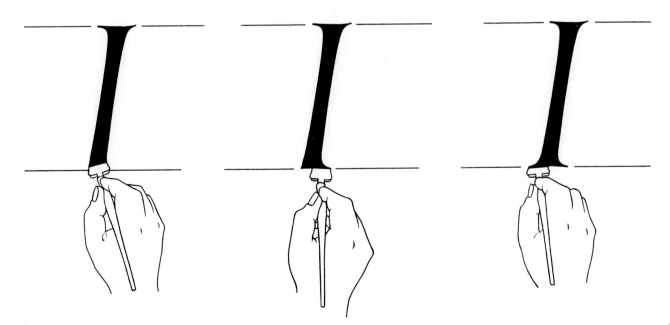

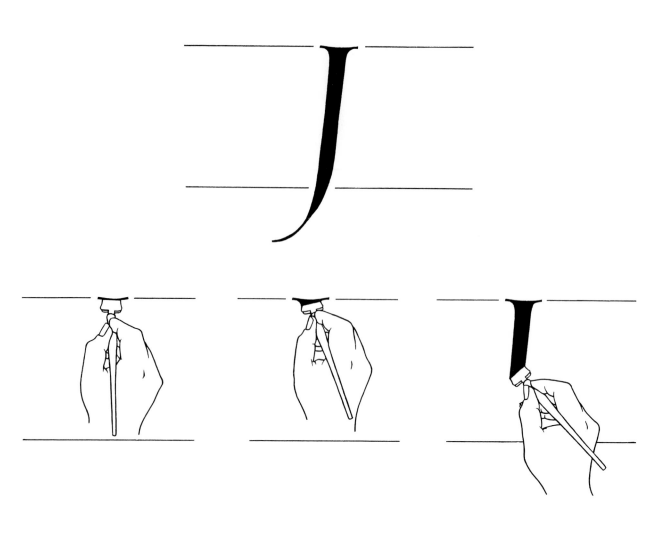

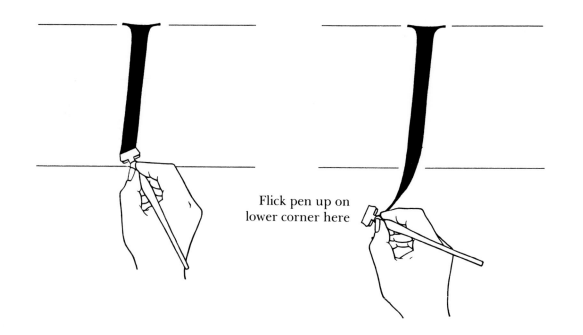

Flick pen up on
lower corner here

K

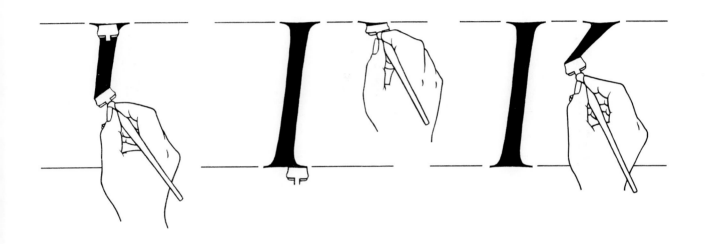

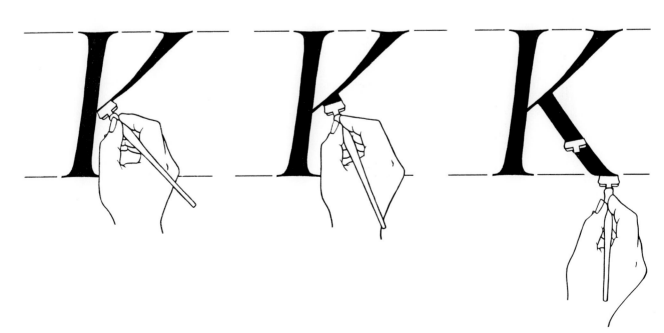

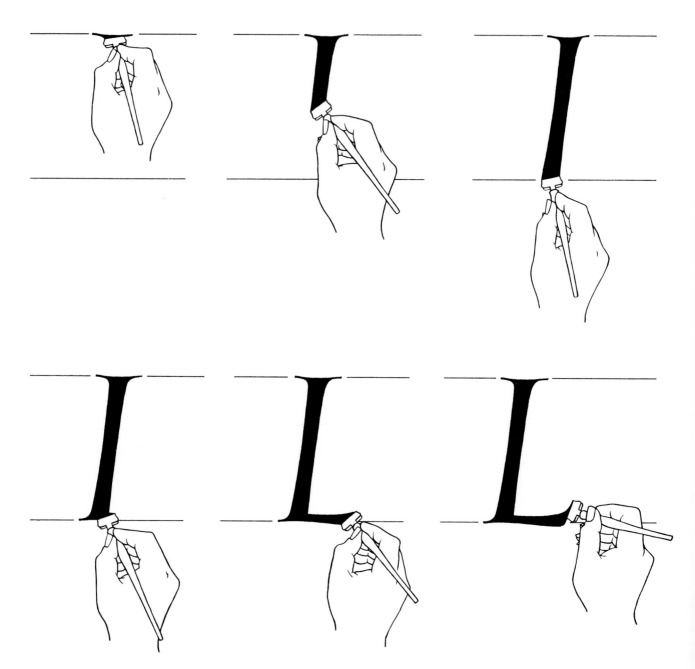

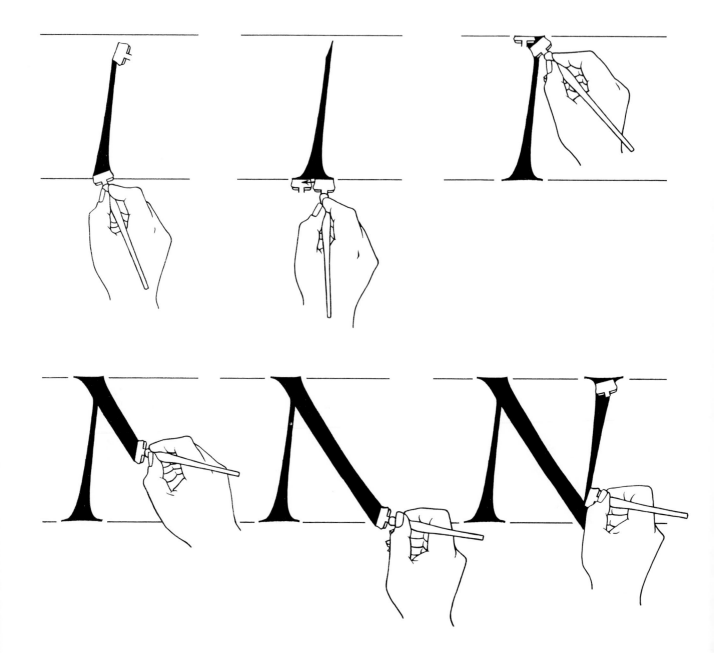

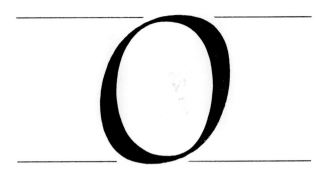

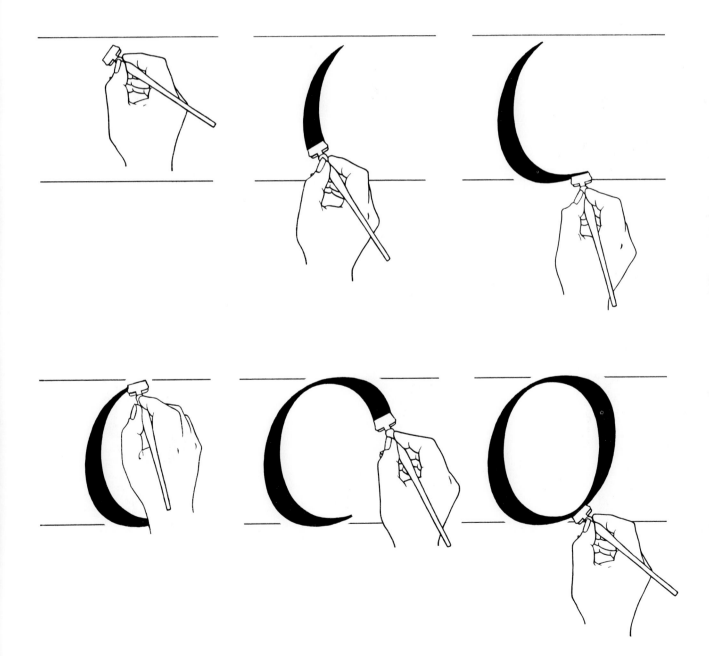

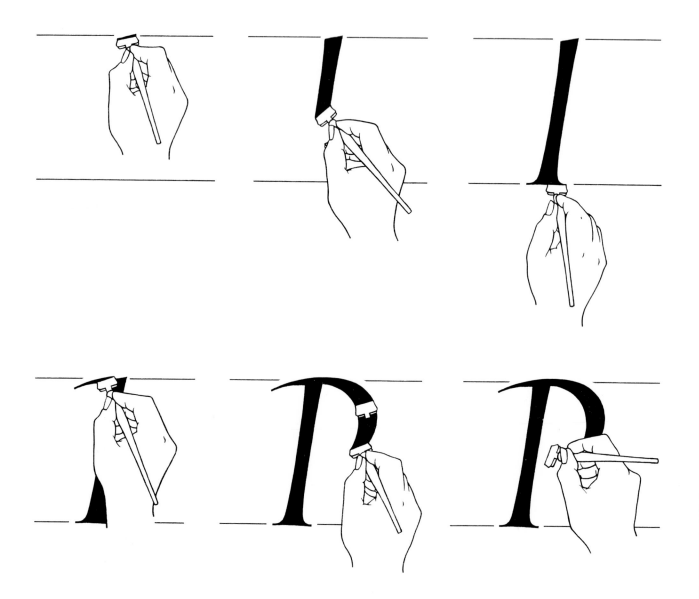

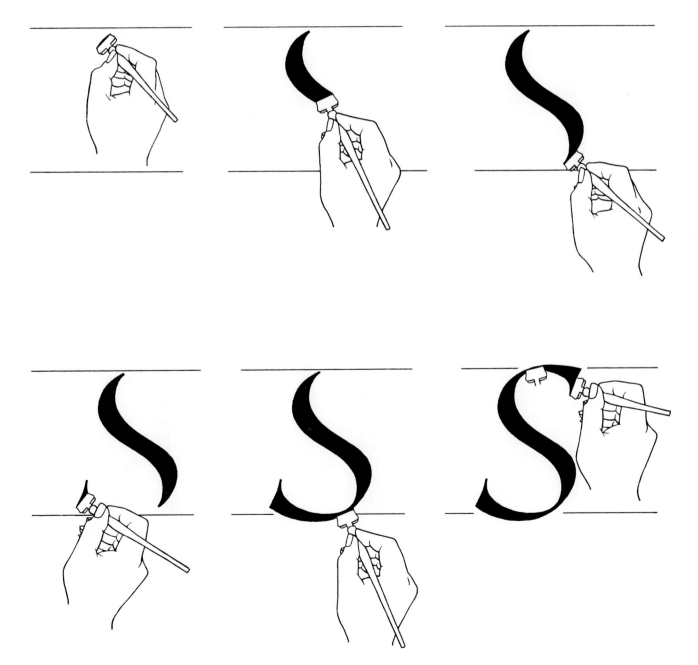

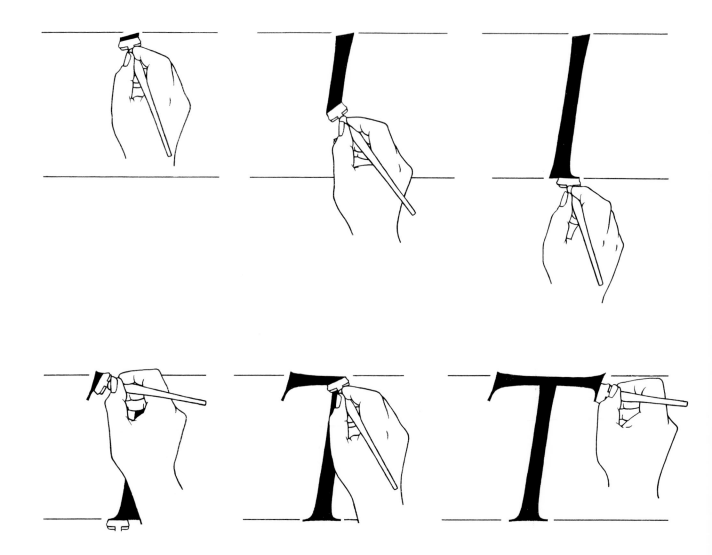

U

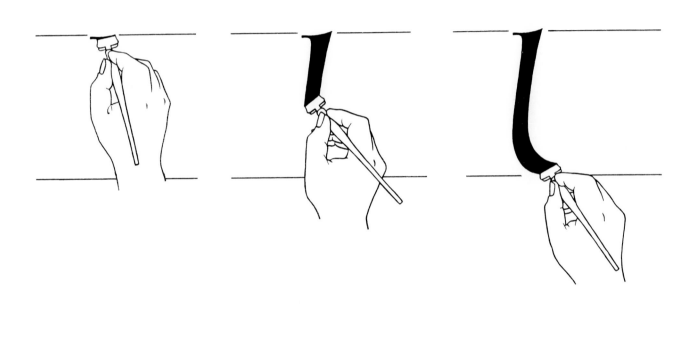

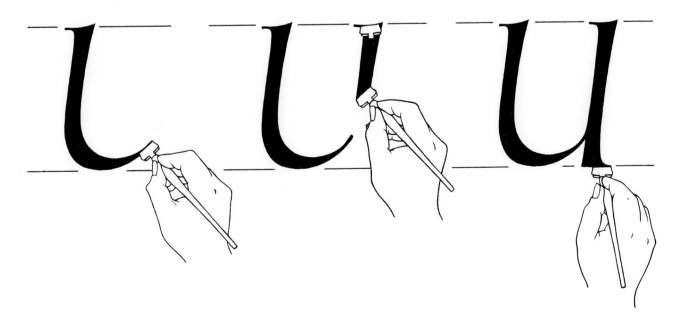

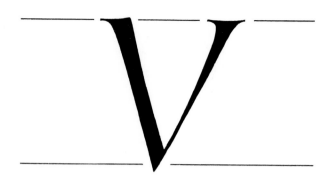

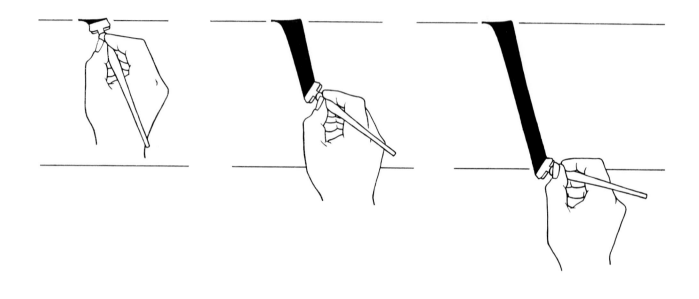

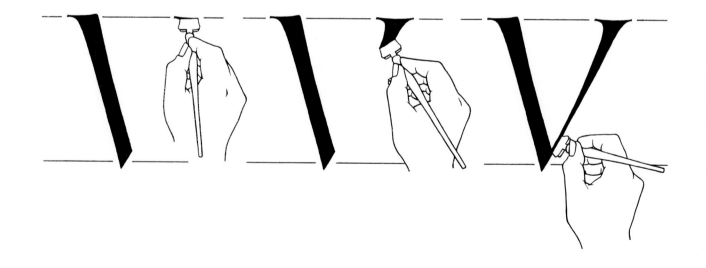

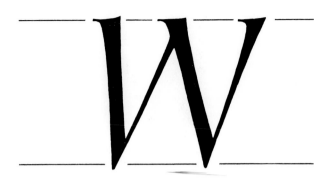

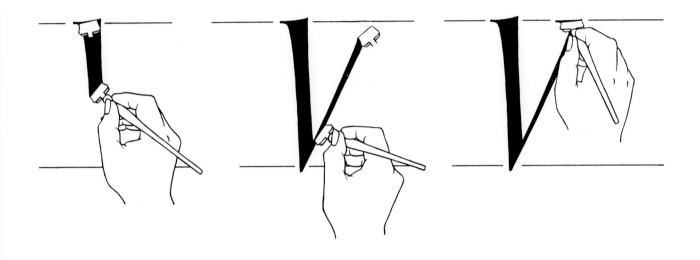

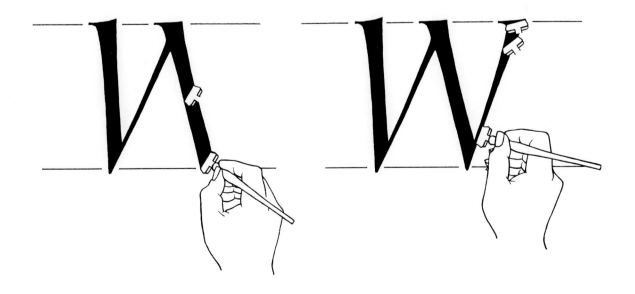

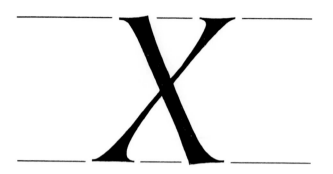

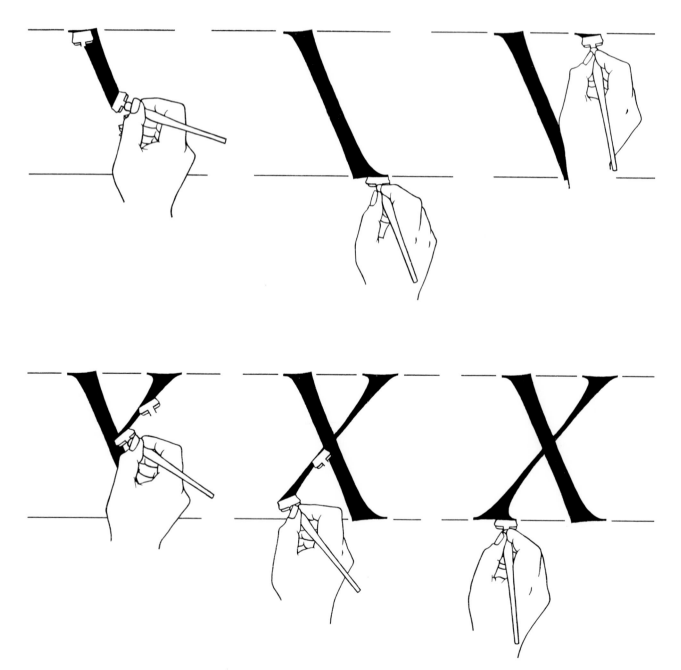

Y

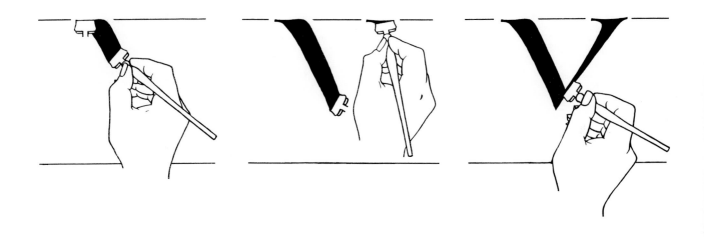

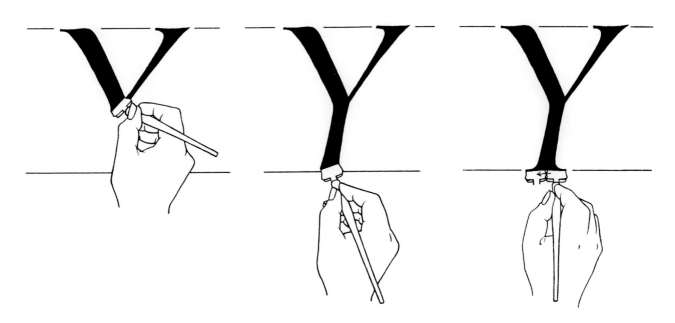

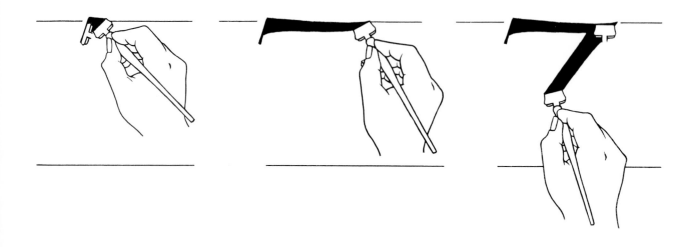

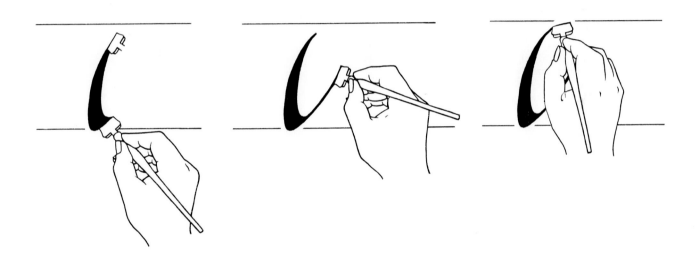

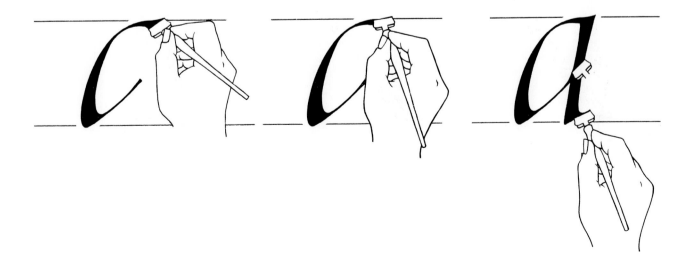

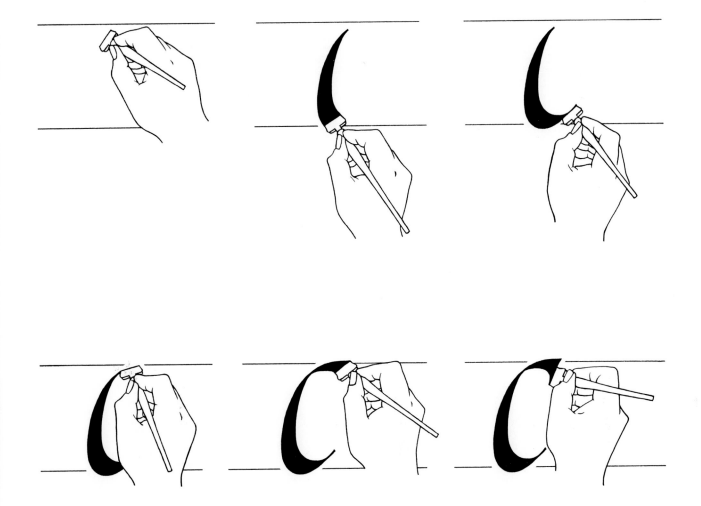

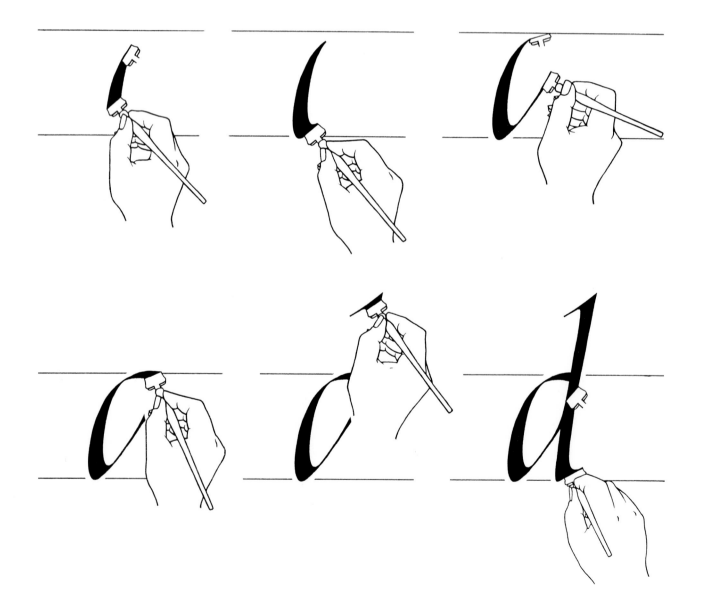

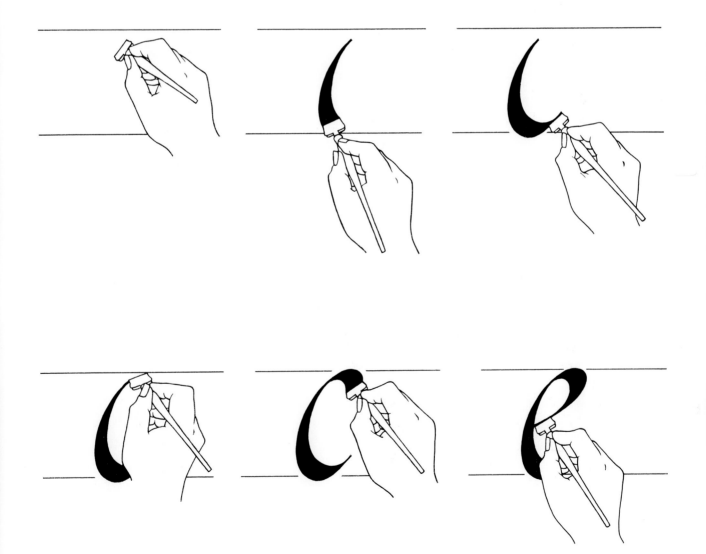

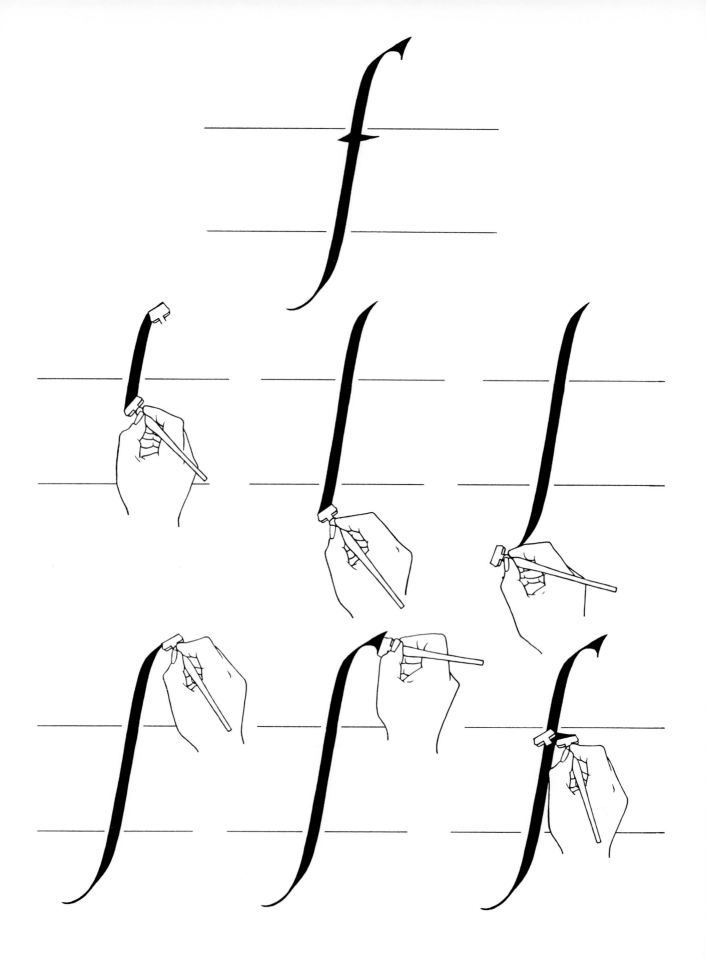

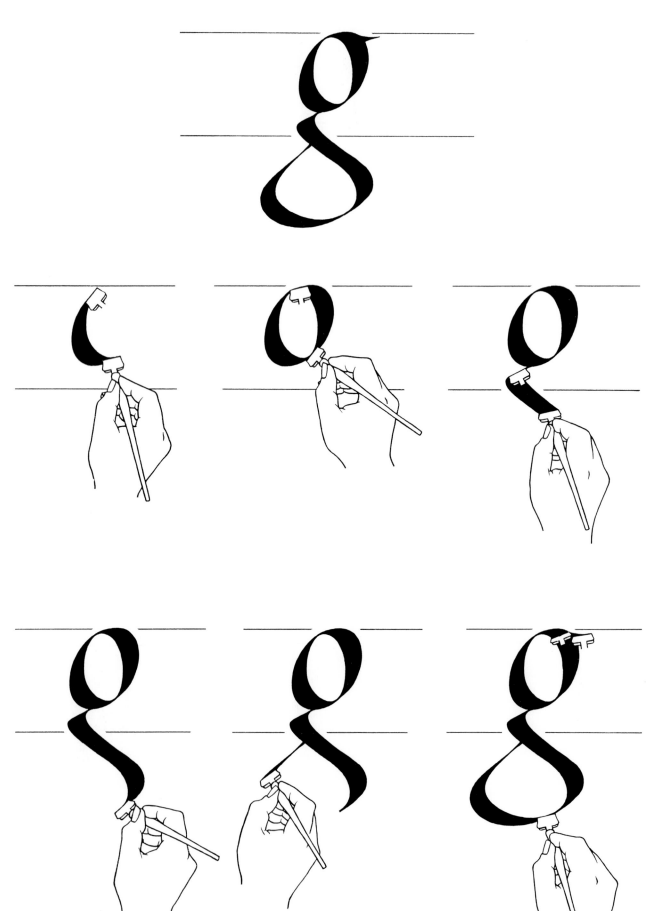

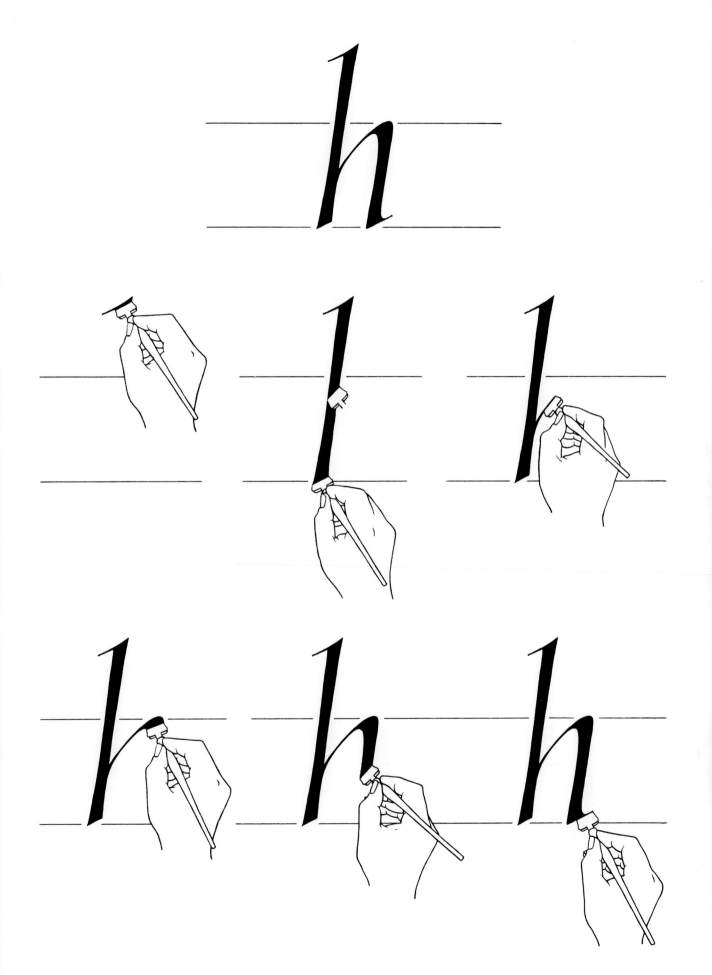

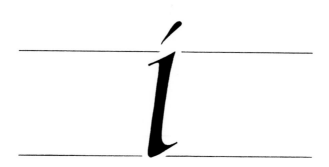

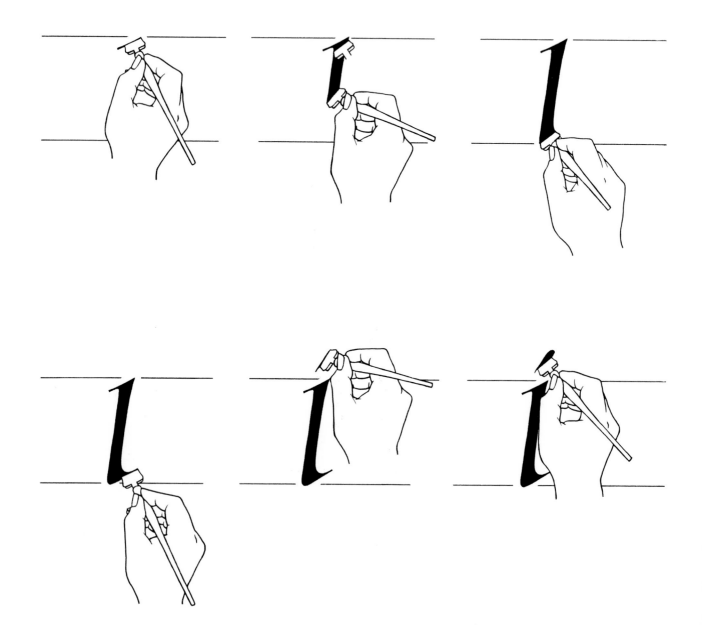

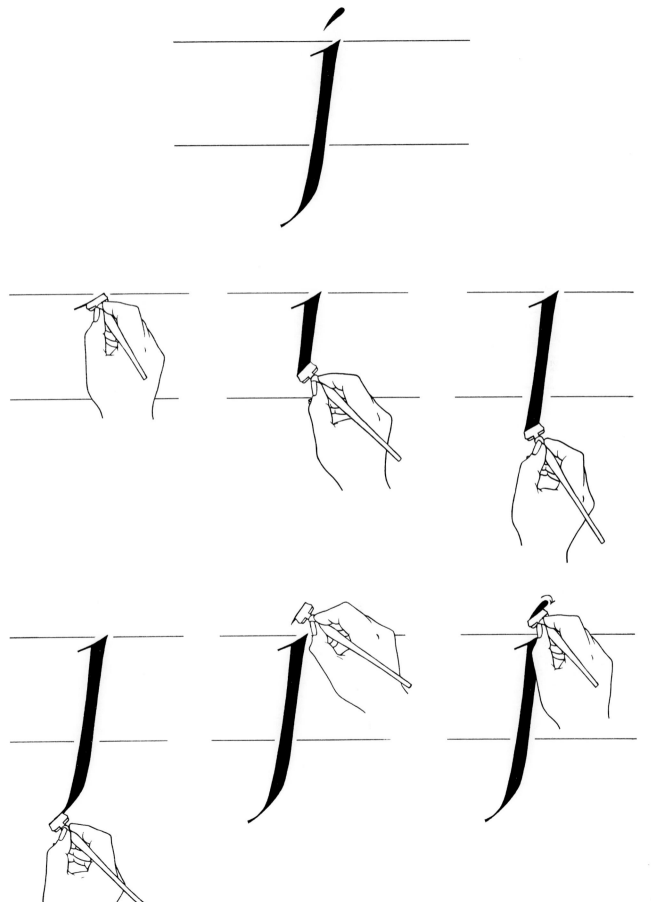

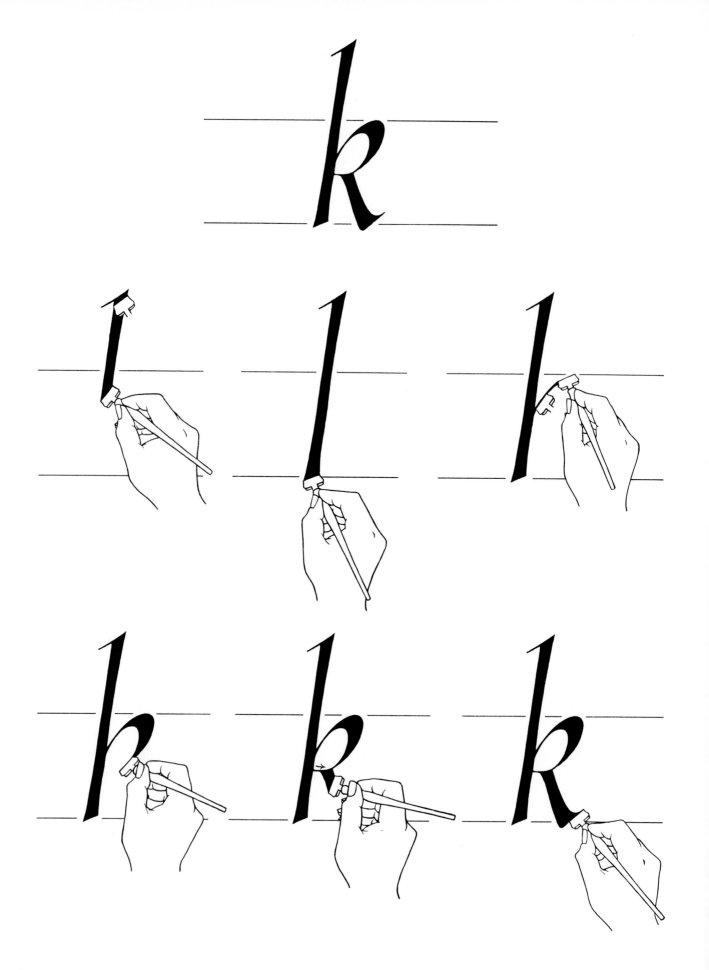

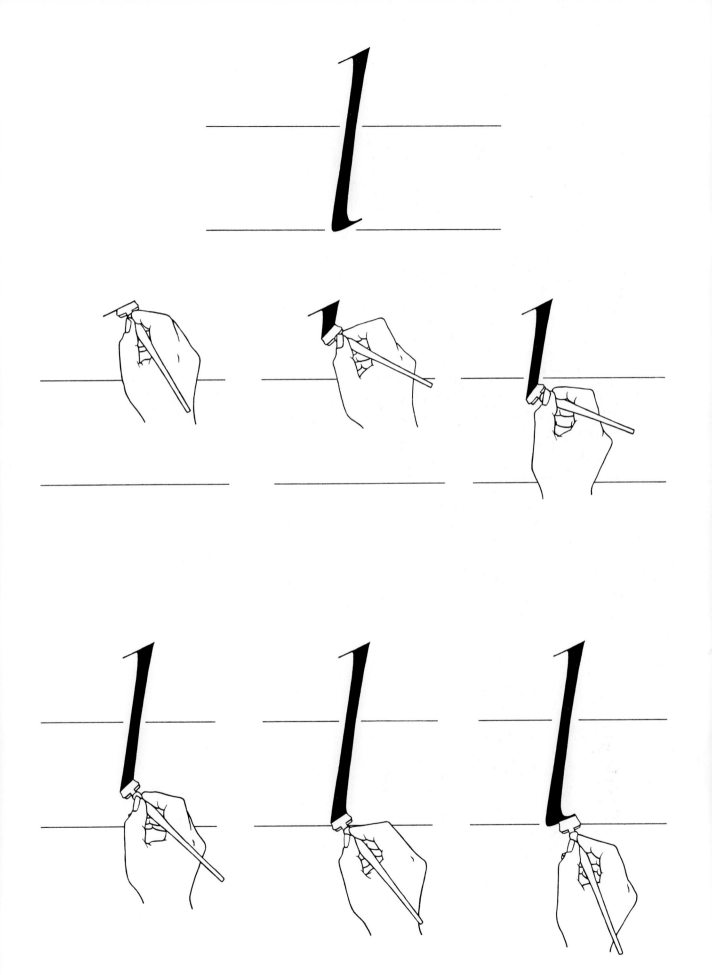

m

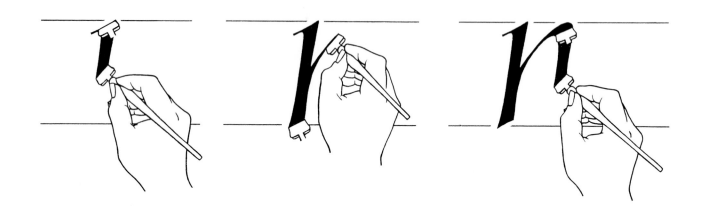

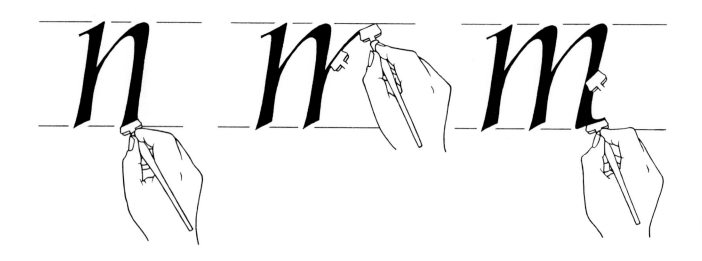

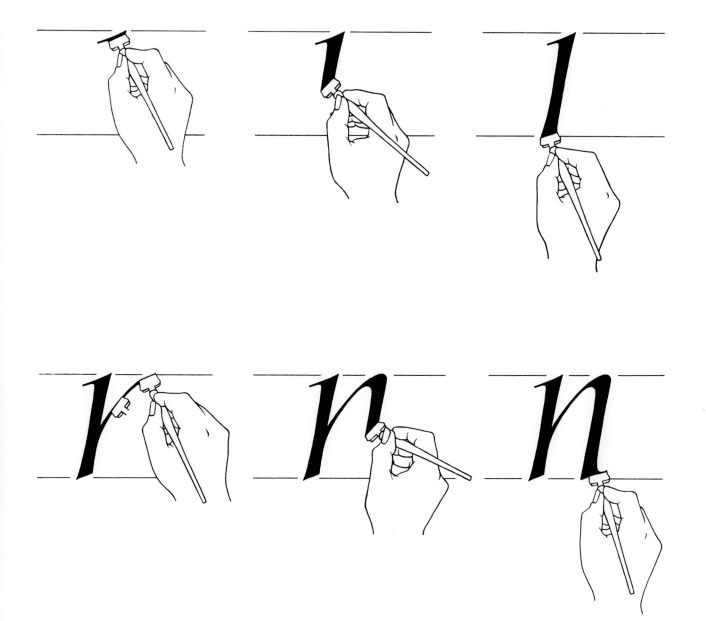

O

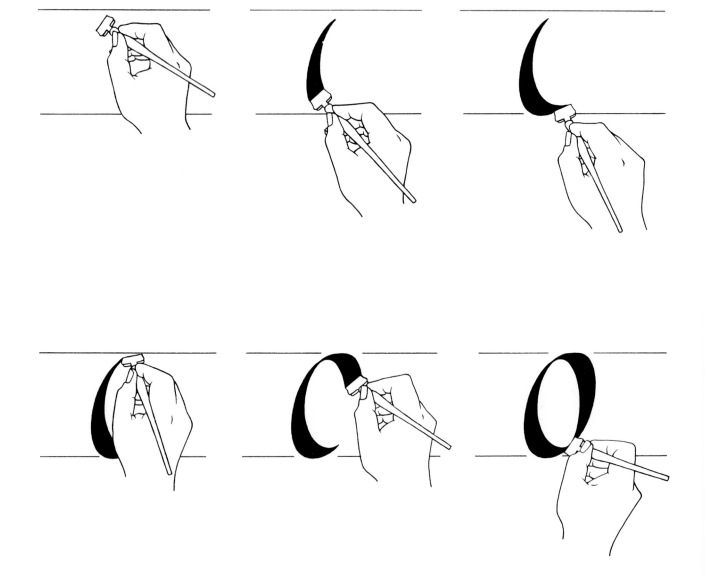

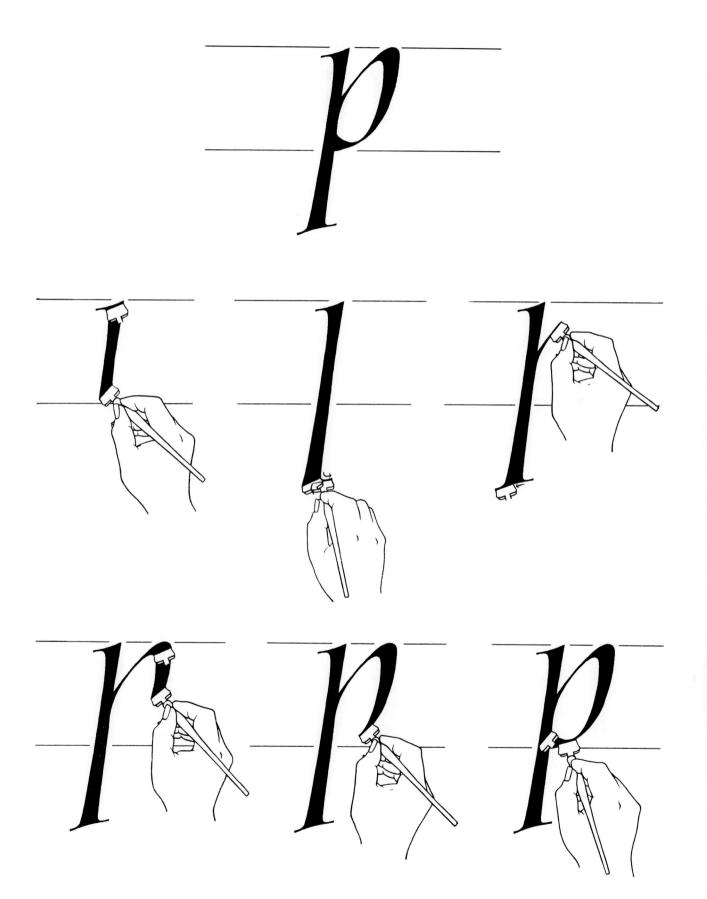

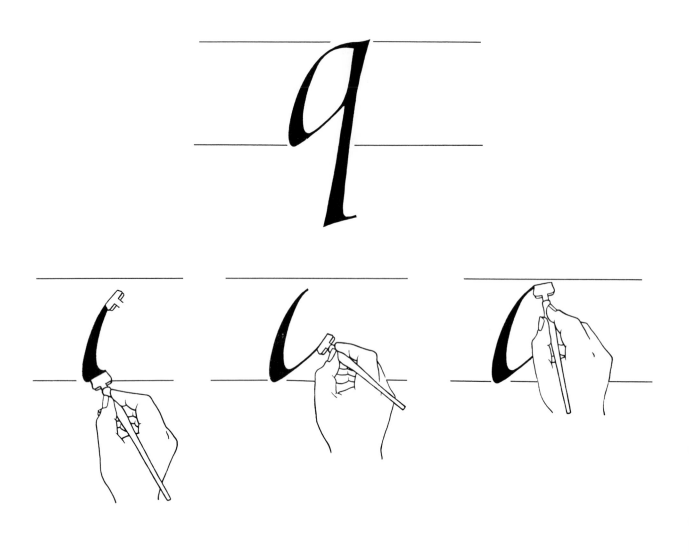

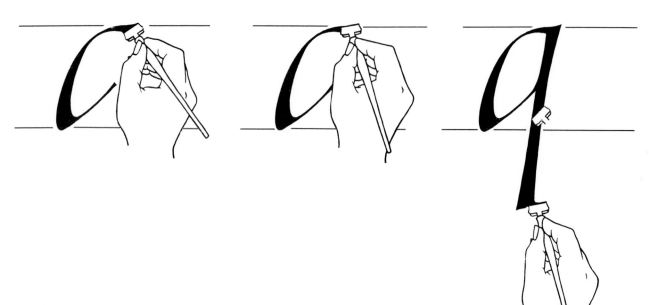

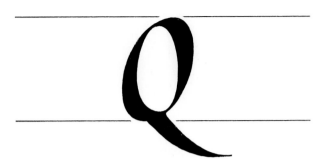

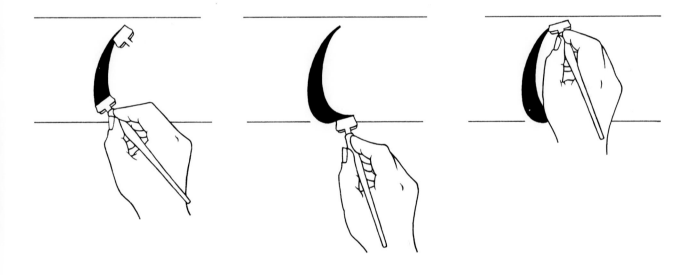

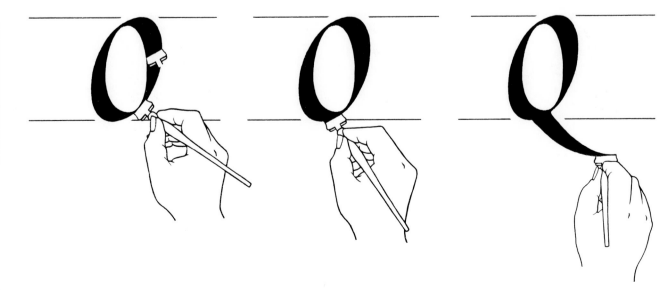

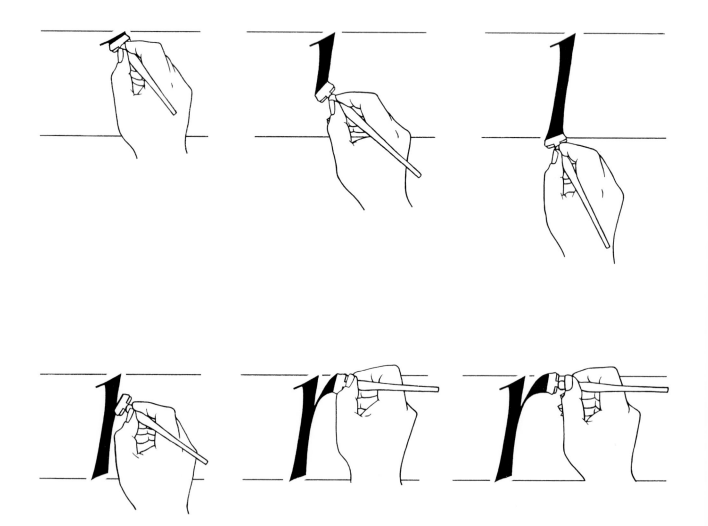

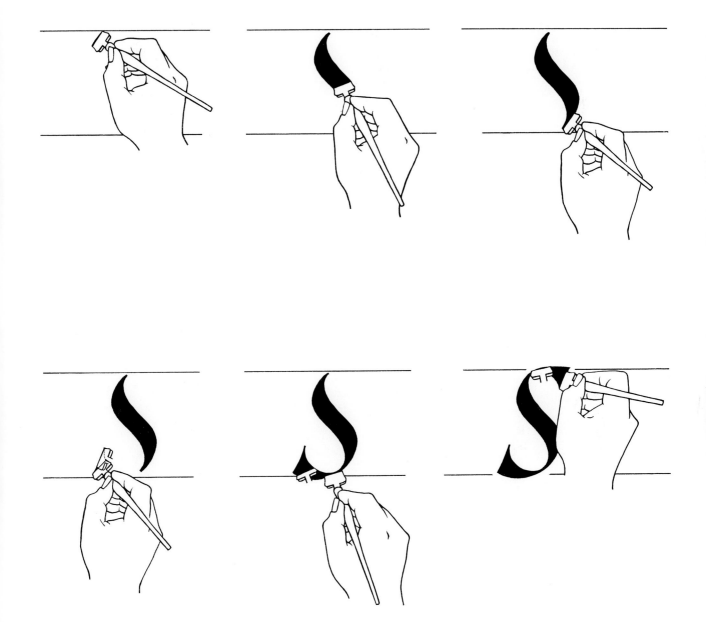

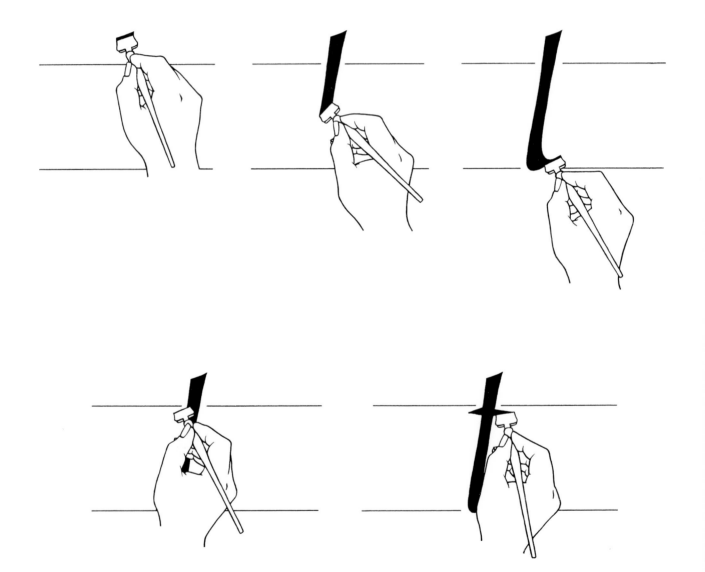

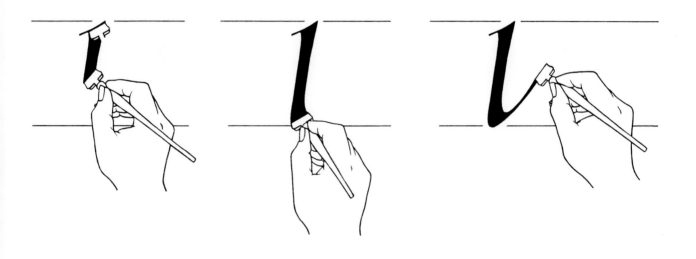

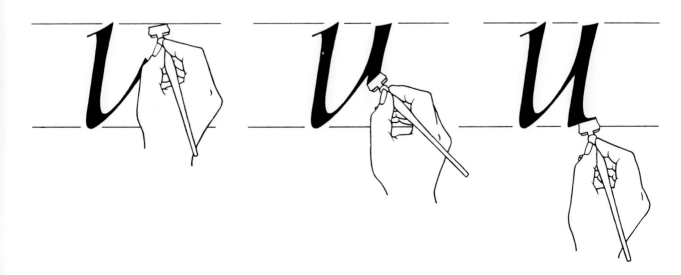

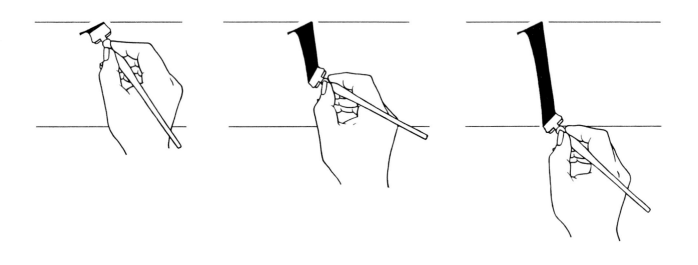

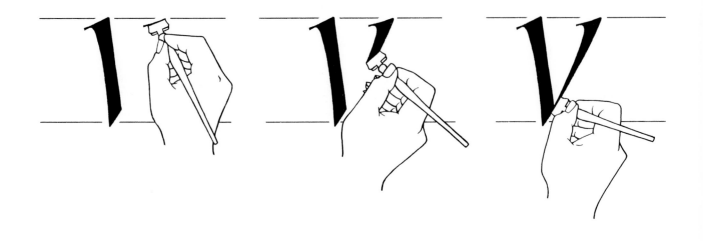

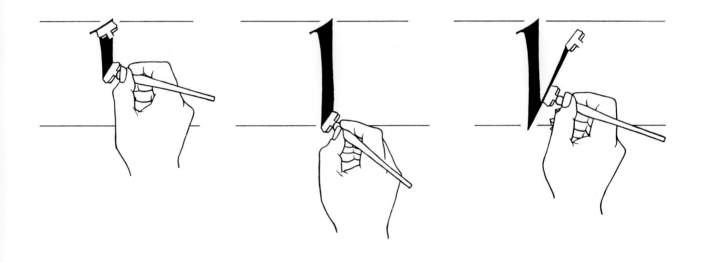

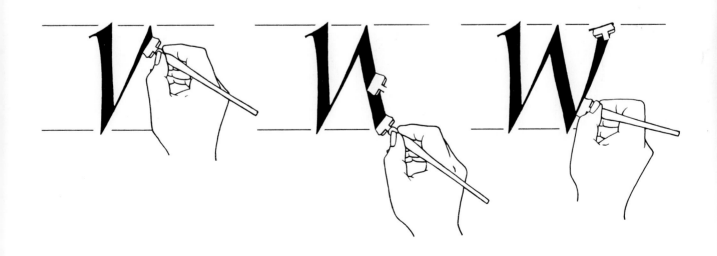

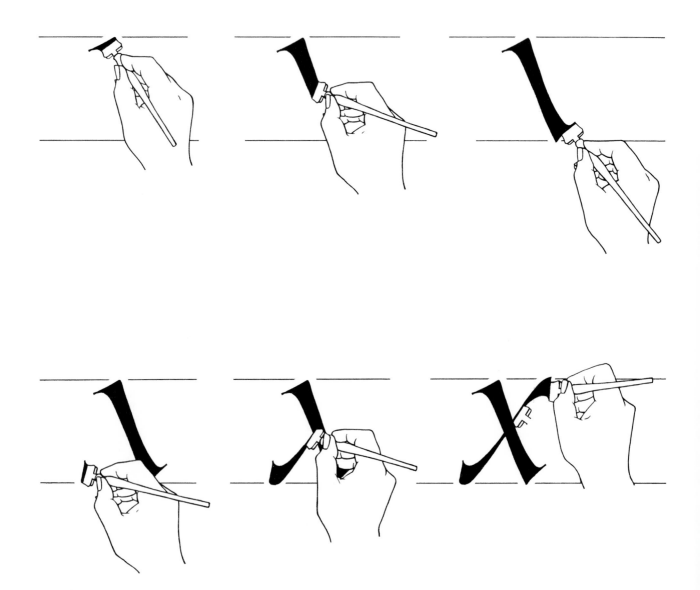

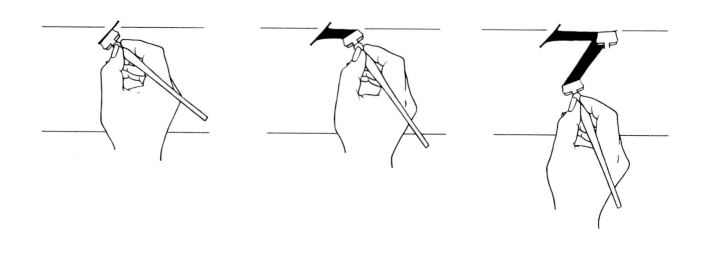

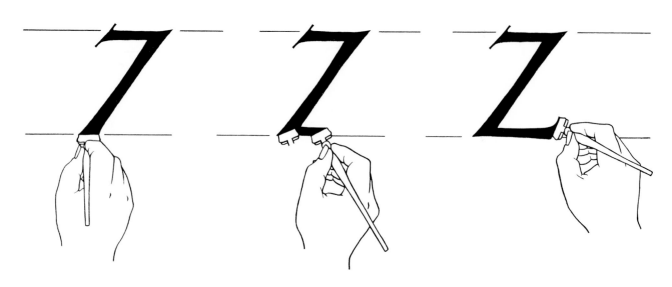

THE PLATES

Aaabbcc

klmnopqr

ABCCDE

LIMNOOI

EFGHIJJK

RSTUVXYZ

ABC
DDEFGHIJKLMN
PQRSTUVWX
YZ

ABAB CcDD

HHIJKKLLM

RRStUVWW

EEFFGGGHI

OOPPQUQ

VXYZIZ

.he commanded, and they were created.

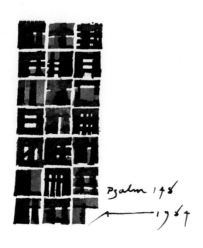

Psalm 148

1964

abcdefghijkl